For You I Write

Let your light so shine before men, that they may see your
good works, and glorify your Father which is in heaven.
Matthew 5:16

For You I Write

"Today, I've decided to use my gifts for You."

For You I Write

But who am I, and who are my people, that we should be
able to give as generously as this? Everything comes from you,
and we have given you only what comes from your hand.
1 Chronicles 29:14

For You I Write

"Today, I've decided to use my gifts for You."

For You I Write

The kingdom of heaven is like a mustard seed that
someone took and sowed in his field. It is the smallest of all
seeds, but when it has grown it is the greatest of
shrubs and becomes a tree.
Matthew 13:31

For You I Write

"Today, I've decided to use my gifts for You."

For You I Write

We have different gifts, according to the grace given us.
If a man's gift is prophesying, let him use
it in proportion to his faith.
Romans 12:8

For You I Write

"Today, I've decided to use my gifts for You."

For You I Write

Show me, O LORD, my life's end and the number of my
days; let me know how fleeting is my life.
Psalm 39:4

For You I Write

"Today, I've decided to use my gifts for You."

For You I Write

I planted the seed, Apollos watered it, but God made it
grow. So neither he who plants nor he who waters is
anything, but only God, who makes things grow.
1 Corinthians 3:6-7

For You I Write

"Today, I've decided to use my gifts for You."

For You I Write

I have brought you glory on earth by completing
the work you gave me to do.
John 17:4

For You I Write

"Today, I've decided to use my gifts for You."

For You I Write

Your hands shaped me and made me.
Job 10:8

For You I Write

"Today, I've decided to use my gifts for You."

For You I Write

...whoever wishes to become great among you must be your servant, and whoever wishes to be first among you must be slave of all. For the Son of Man came not to be served, and to give his life a ransom for many.
Mark 10:43-45

For You I Write

"Today, I've decided to use my gifts for You."

For You I Write

Blessed are those who have not seen
And yet have come to believe.
John 20:29

For You I Write

"Today, I've decided to use my gifts for You."

For You I Write

But strive first for the kingdom of God and his righteousness,
and all these things will be given to you as well.
Matthew 6:33

For You I Write

"Today, I've decided to use my gifts for You."

For You I Write

Now to him who by the power at work within
us is able to accomplish abundantly far
more than we can ask or imagine.
Ephesians 3:20

For You I Write

"Today, I've decided to use my gifts for You."

For You I Write

I knew your works; you are neither cold not hot.
I wish that you were either cold or hot. So, because you are
lukewarm, and neither cold not hot, I am about to spit you
out of my mouth. Revelation 3:15-16

For You I Write

"Today, I've decided to use my gifts for You."

For You I Write

The good person out of the good treasure of the heart
produces good, and the evil person out of the evil
treasure produces evil; for it is out of the abundance
of the heart that the mouth speaks.
Luke 6:45

For You I Write

"Today, I've decided to use my gifts for You."

For You I Write

Either make the tree good, and it's fruit good, or make the
tree bad, and its fruit bad; for the tree is known by its fruit.
Matthew 12:33

For You I Write

"Today, I've decided to use my gifts for You."

For You I Write

I have fought the good fight. I have finished the race.
I have kept the faith.
2 Timothy 4:7

For You I Write

"Today, I've decided to use my gifts for You."

For You I Write

Whatever your task, put yourselves into it, as done
for the Lord and not for your masters.
Colossians 3:23

For You I Write

"Today, I've decided to use my gifts for You."

For You I Write

Be doers of the world, and not merely hearers
who deceive themselves.
James 1:22

For You I Write

"Today, I've decided to use my gifts for You."

For You I Write

For it is God who is at work in you, enabling you both to will
and to work for his good pleasure.
Philippians 2:13

For You I Write

"Today, I've decided to use my gifts for You."

For You I Write

In him we were also chosen, having been predestined
according to the plan of him who works out everything in
conformity with the purpose of his will, in order that we,
who were the first to hope in Christ, might be
for the praise of his glory.
Ephesians 1:11-12

For You I Write

"Today, I've decided to use my gifts for You."

For You I Write

We will not hide them from their children; we will tell the
next generation the praiseworthy deeds of the Lord, his
power, and the wonders he has done.
Psalm 78:4

For You I Write

"Today, I've decided to use my gifts for You."

For You I Write

Whoever trusts in his riches will fall, but the
righteous will thrive like a green leaf.
Proverbs 11:28

For You I Write

"Today, I've decided to use my gifts for You."

For You I Write

But blessed is the man who trusts in the Lord, whose
confidence is in him. He will be like a tree planted by the
water that sends out its roots by the stream. It does not fear
when heat comes; its leaves are always green.
Jeremiah 17:7-8

For You I Write

"Today, I've decided to use my gifts for You."

For You I Write

I will sacrifice a freewill offering to you; I will
praise your name, O LORD, for it is good.
Psalm 54:6

For You I Write

"Today, I've decided to use my gifts for You."

For You I Write

For by him all things were created: things in heaven and
on earth, visible and invisible, whether thrones or
powers or rulers or authorities; all things
were created by him and for him.
Colossians 1:16

For You I Write

"Today, I've decided to use my gifts for You."

For You I Write

God works through different men in different ways, but is
the same God who achieves his purpose through them all.
1 Corinthians 12:6

For You I Write

"Today, I've decided to use my gifts for You."

For You I Write

Or do you not know that your body is a temple of the Holy
Spirit within you, whom you have from God? You are not
your own, for you were bought with a price.
So glorify God in your body. 1 Corinthians 6:19-20

For You I Write

"Today, I've decided to use my gifts for You."

For You I Write

This world is fading away, along with everything that it
craves. But if you do the will of God, you will live forever.
1 John 2:17

For You I Write

"Today, I've decided to use my gifts for You."

For You I Write

We understand what love is when we realize that Christ
gave his life for us. That means we must
give our lives for other believers.
1 John 3:16

For You I Write

"Today, I've decided to use my gifts for You."

For You I Write

And this is our confidence, that if we pray according to His
will, He will hear us, and give us what we ask for, because
our desires are in agreement with His thoughts for us.
1 John 5:14-15

For You I Write

"Today, I've decided to use my gifts for You."

For You I Write

God has given each of you some special abilities; be sure
to use them to help each other, passing on to
others God's many kinds of blessings.
1 Peter 4:10

For You I Write

"Today, I've decided to use my gifts for You."

For You I Write

Everything got started in him and finds its purpose in him.
Colossians 1:16

For You I Write

"Today, I've decided to use my gifts for You."

For You I Write

To everything there is a season, and a time for
every matter or purpose under heaven.
Ecclesiastes 3:1

For You I Write

"Today, I've decided to use my gifts for You."

For You I Write

For we are God's workmanship, created in Christ Jesus to do
good works, which God prepared in advance for us to do.
Ephesians 2:10

For You I Write

"Today, I've decided to use my gifts for You."

For You I Write

For by grace you have been saved through faith. And this
is not your own doing; it is the gift of God, not a
result of works, so that no one may boast.
Ephesians 2:8-9

For You I Write

"Today, I've decided to use my gifts for You."

For You I Write

Live life with a due sense of responsibility, not as those who
do not know the meaning of life but as those who do.
Ephesians 5:15

For You I Write

"Today, I've decided to use my gifts for You."

For You I Write

O Lord, you are my God; I will exalt you and praise your
name, for in perfect faithfulness you have done
marvelous things, things planned long ago.
Isaiah 25: 1

For You I Write

"Today, I've decided to use my gifts for You."

For You I Write

You, Lord, give perfect peace to those who keep
their purpose firm and put their trust in You.
Isaiah 26:3

For You I Write

"Today, I've decided to use my gifts for You."

For You I Write

Draw close to God, and God will draw close to you.
James 4:8

For You I Write

"Today, I've decided to use my gifts for You."

For You I Write

You did not choose me, but I chose you and appointed you that you should go and bear fruit and that your fruit should abide, so that whatever you ask the Father in my name, he may give it to you. John 15:16

For You I Write

"Today, I've decided to use my gifts for You."

For You I Write

For I have come down from heaven not to do My own will and
purpose but to do the will and purpose of Him Who sent Me.
John 6: 38

For You I Write

"Today, I've decided to use my gifts for You."

For You I Write

Unless you are faithful in small matters, you
will not be faithful in large ones.
Luke 16:10

For You I Write

"Today, I've decided to use my gifts for You."

For You I Write

Love the Lord your God with all your heart and with all your
soul and with all your mind and with all your strength.
Mark 12:30

For You I Write

"Today, I've decided to use my gifts for You."

For You I Write

If you give even a cup of cold water to one of the least
of my followers, you will surely be rewarded.
Matthew 10:42

For You I Write

"Today, I've decided to use my gifts for You."

For You I Write

God began doing a good work in you, and I am sure he will
continue it until it is finished when Jesus Christ comes again.
Philippians 1:6

For You I Write

"Today, I've decided to use my gifts for You."

For You I Write

The heart of man plans his way,
but the Lord establishes his steps.
Proverbs 16:9

For You I Write

"Today, I've decided to use my gifts for You."

For You I Write

Many plans are in a man's mind, but it is the
Lord's purpose for him that will stand.
Proverbs 19: 21

For You I Write

"Today, I've decided to use my gifts for You."

For You I Write

Your word is a lamp to my feet, and a light to my path.
Psalm 119:105

For You I Write

"Today, I've decided to use my gifts for You."

For You I Write

For everything comes from God alone. Everything
lives by his power, and everything is for His glory.
Romans 11:36

For You I Write

"Today, I've decided to use my gifts for You."

For You I Write

Whoever finds his life will lose it, and whoever
loses his life for my sake will find it.
Matthew 10:39

For You I Write

"Today, I've decided to use my gifts for You."

For You I Write

Let God transform you inwardly by a complete change of
your mind. Then you will be able to know the will of God -
what is good and is pleasing to Him and is perfect.
Romans 12:2

For You I Write

"Today, I've decided to use my gifts for You."

For You I Write

Surrender your whole being to Him
to be used for righteous purposes.
Romans 6:13

For You I Write

"Today, I've decided to use my gifts for You."

For You I Write

And we know that God causes all things to work together
for good to those who love Him, to enable them to
fulfill the purpose for which they are called.
Romans 8:28

For You I Write

"Today, I've decided to use my gifts for You."

For You I Write

And do not be conformed to this world, but be
transformed by the renewing of your mind, that you may
prove what the will of God is, that which is good and
acceptable and perfect. Romans 12:2

For You I Write

"Today, I've decided to use my gifts for You."

For You I Write

No one can serve two masters. Either he will hate the one
and love the other, or he will be devoted to the one and
despise the other. You cannot serve both God and Money.
Matthew 6:24

For You I Write

"Today, I've decided to use my gifts for You."

For You I Write

For I know the plans I have for you, declares the Lord, plans
to prosper you and not to harm you, plans
to give you hope and a future.
Jeremiah 29:11

For You I Write

"Today, I've decided to use my gifts for You."

For You I Write

Now to Him who is able to do exceeding abundantly
beyond all that we ask or think, according
to the power that works within us...
Ephesians 3:20

For You I Write

"Today, I've decided to use my gifts for You."

For You I Write

I can do all things through Christ who strengthens me.
Philippians 4:13

For You I Write

"Today, I've decided to use my gifts for You."

For You I Write

However, I consider my life worth nothing to me,
if only I may finish the race and complete the task
the Lord Jesus has given me--the task of testifying
to the gospel of God's grace. Acts 20:24

For You I Write

"Today, I've decided to use my gifts for You."

For You I Write

His master said to him, 'Well done, good and faithful slave;
you were faithful with a few things, I will put you in charge
of many things, enter into the joy of your master.'
Matthew 25:21

For You I Write

"Today, I've decided to use my gifts for You."

For You I Write

But the one who does not know and does things deserving
punishment will be beaten with few blows. From everyone
who has been given much, much will be demanded; and
from the one who has been entrusted with much,
much more will be asked. Luke 12:48

For You I Write

"Today, I've decided to use my gifts for You."

For You I Write

The heavens are telling of the glory of God; And their
expanse is declaring the work of His hands.
Psalm 19:1

For You I Write

"Today, I've decided to use my gifts for You."

For You I Write

I glorified Thee on the earth, having accomplished
the work which Thou hast given Me to do.
John 17:4

For You I Write

"Today, I've decided to use my gifts for You."

For You I Write

I will bless the Lord at all times; His praise
shall continually be in my mouth.
Psalm 34:1

For You I Write

"Today, I've decided to use my gifts for You."

For You I Write

Whether, then, you eat or drink or whatever
you do, do all to the glory of God.
1 Corinthians 10:31

For You I Write

"Today, I've decided to use my gifts for You."

For You I Write

And whatever you do, do it heartily, as to the Lord and not
to men, knowing that from the Lord you will receive the
reward of the inheritance; for you serve the Lord Christ.
Colossians 3:23-24

For You I Write

"Today, I've decided to use my gifts for You."

For You I Write

Whoever watches the wind will not plant;
whoever looks at the clouds will not reap.
Ecclesiastes 11:4

For You I Write

"Today, I've decided to use my gifts for You."

For You I Write

Do not neglect your gift, which was given you through a
prophetic message when the body of
elders laid their hands on you.
1 Timothy 4:14

For You I Write

"Today, I've decided to use my gifts for You."

For You I Write

And without faith it is impossible to please Him, for he who
comes to God must believe that He is, and that He
is a rewarder of those who seek Him.
Hebrews 11:6

For You I Write

"Today, I've decided to use my gifts for You."

For You I Write

You see that a man is justified by works,
and not by faith alone.
James 2:24

For You I Write

"Today, I've decided to use my gifts for You."

For You I Write

But seek first his kingdom and his righteousness,
and all these things will be given to you as well.
Matthew 6:33

For You I Write

"Today, I've decided to use my gifts for You."

For You I Write

And He was saying to them all, If anyone wishes to come
after Me, let him deny himself, and take up
his cross daily, and follow Me.
Luke 9:23

For You I Write

"Today, I've decided to use my gifts for You."

For You I Write

By their fruit you will recognize them. Do people pick
grapes from thorn bushes, or figs from thistles?
Matthew 7:16

For You I Write

"Today, I've decided to use my gifts for You."

For You I Write

Blessed is a man who perseveres under trial; for once he
has been approved, he will receive the crown of life, which
the Lord has promised to those who love Him.
James 1:12

For You I Write

"Today, I've decided to use my gifts for You."

For You I Write

My grace is sufficient for you, for my power
is made perfect in weakness.
2 Corinthians 12:9

For You I Write

"Today, I've decided to use my gifts for You."

For You I Write

Still other seed fell on good soil. It came up,
grew and produced a crop, multiplying
thirty, sixty, or even a hundred times.
Mark 4:8

For You I Write

"Today, I've decided to use my gifts for You."

For You I Write

Everything comes from you, and we have given
you only what comes from your hand.
1 Chronicles 29:14

For You I Write

"Today, I've decided to use my gifts for You."

For You I Write

As long as it is day, we must do the work of Him who sent
me. Night is coming, when no one can work.
John 9:4

For You I Write

"Today, I've decided to use my gifts for You."

For You I Write

Jesus replied, "No one who puts his hand to the plow and
looks back is fit for service in the kingdom of God."
Luke 9:62

For You I Write

"Today, I've decided to use my gifts for You."

For You I Write

He said to them, "Go into all the world and
preach the good news to all creation."
Mark 16:15

For You I Write

"Today, I've decided to use my gifts for You."

www.ingramcontent.com/pod-product-compliance
Lightning Source LLC
Chambersburg PA
CBHW030514100426

42813CB00001B/36